AF269505

CHINESE MYTHOLOGY

Xiwangmu
Queen Mother of the West

BY SAMANTHA S. BELL

CONTENT CONSULTANT
GANG LIU, PhD
ASSOCIATE TEACHING PROFESSOR
CARNEGIE MELLON UNIVERSITY

Kids Core
An Imprint of Abdo Publishing
abdobooks.com

abdobooks.com

Published by Abdo Publishing, a division of ABDO, PO Box 398166, Minneapolis, Minnesota 55439. Copyright © 2023 by Abdo Consulting Group, Inc. International copyrights reserved in all countries. No part of this book may be reproduced in any form without written permission from the publisher. Kids Core™ is a trademark and logo of Abdo Publishing.

Printed in the United States of America, North Mankato, Minnesota.
102022
012023

THIS BOOK CONTAINS
RECYCLED MATERIALS

Cover Photo: Interfoto/Fine Arts/Alamy
Interior Photos: Alamy, 4–5, 29 (top); Sepia Times/Universal Images Group/Getty Images, 6, 10, 14, 28 (bottom); Heritage Art/Heritage Images/Hulton Archive/Getty Images, 9, 23, 28 (top); Pictures from History/Universal Images Group/Getty Images, 12–13, 26; Red Line Editorial, 17; Alexander L. S./Shutterstock Images, 18; Godong/Universal Images Group/Getty Images, 20–21; Museum of East Asian Art/Heritage Images/Hulton Archive/Getty Images, 22; Mark Brandon/Shutterstock Images, 24, 29 (bottom)

Editor: Ann Schwab
Series Designer: Ryan Gale

Library of Congress Control Number: 2022940690

Publisher's Cataloging-in-Publication Data

Names: Bell, Samantha S., author.
Title: Xiwangmu: Queen Mother of the West / by Samantha S. Bell
Description: Minneapolis, Minnesota: Abdo Publishing, 2023 | Series: Chinese Mythology | Includes online
     resources and index.
Identifiers: ISBN 9781532199981 (lib. bdg.) | ISBN 9781098275181 (ebook)
Subjects: LCSH: Deities--Juvenile literature. | Gods, Chinese--Juvenile literature. | Mythology, Chinese--
     Juvenile literature.
Classification: DDC 299.51--dc23

CONTENTS

Xiwangmu, *center*, hosts a banquet for gods and goddesses every 3,000 years.

A Feast for the Gods

Xiwangmu lives high in the snowy Kunlun Mountains. Her palace is made of gold, jade, and precious stones. Every 3,000 years, Xiwangmu holds a banquet. It is called the Feast of Peaches.

Dongfang Shuo worked for the emperor. But after eating the peaches he stole from Xiwangmu, Dongfang became immortal.

The banquet is for **immortals**, those beings who will never die. Guests dine on peaches from Xiwangmu's orchard. The peach trees produce fruit once every 3,000 years. Those who eat the peaches will become immortal for 3,000 more years. The guests also celebrate

Xiwangmu's birthday. The festive event includes singing and music from invisible instruments.

Once Xiwangmu gave five peaches to the emperor of China. The emperor wanted to plant the seeds and grow his own fruit. But Xiwangmu told him he would have to wait 3,000 years for more peaches.

Stealing Immortality

Dongfang Shuo was a priest and an official at the court of Han emperor Wu. This emperor ruled China from 141–87 BCE. When Dongfang was visiting heaven, he stole some peaches. Xiwangmu had planted them for the Jade Emperor, Yudi. Dongfang ate the peaches and became immortal.

Xiwangmu, also spelled Hsi Wang Mu, means "Queen Mother of the West." She is also called the Golden Mother of the Tortoise. The tortoise represents long life and immortality.

Stories for Everyone

The story of Xiwangmu and the Feast of Peaches is called a myth. Some Chinese myths tell about gods and goddesses. Others explain religious or **cultural** traditions. Some tell about the history of groups of people. Still others are told just for entertainment.

Xiwangmu, *left*, has been called many different names throughout history. She is sometimes called the Golden Mother or the Divine Mother.

In Chinese myths, cranes and the peaches that
grow in Xiwangmu's garden represent a long life.

Chinese myths may be written as stories, poems, or songs. They go back as far as the 1100s BCE. Some people believe certain myths are true. Others think parts of the stories may be true. Still others think no part of the myths happened. But people agree that the myths teach lessons for life.

Explore Online

Visit the website below. Does it give any new information about the Peaches of Immortality that wasn't in Chapter One?

"Peach of Immortality" in Chinese Mythology

abdocorelibrary.com/xiwangmu

Xiwangmu is known as an important and powerful goddess.

CHAPTER 2

Goddess of Immortality

In the myths, Xiwangmu changed over time. In the earliest stories, she had a panther's tail and a tiger's teeth. She lived in a rocky cave in a jade mountain. Three green birds brought her food.

She was fierce and very powerful. She controlled punishments, plagues, and other disasters.

In later myths, Xiwangmu looked more human. She had also become much more powerful. Xiwangmu joined the Lord of the East, Dongwanggong. Together they brought everything to life. Xiwangmu was considered the **ancestor** of the gods and goddesses.

During the Han dynasty (about 206 BCE–220 CE), people worshipped her as the goddess of wealth, health, **calamity**, and immortality. She communicated through poetry and songs. By the time of the Tang dynasty (618 CE–907 CE), Xiwangmu had become the beautiful ruler of heaven. She took care of her garden as the Keeper of the Peaches of Immortality.

Opposites in the Heavens

According to some beliefs, all the forces in nature are either yin or yang. They are opposites. Yin represents darkness, cold, slowness, and female energy. Yang represents brightness, heat, movement, and male energy. Over time, Xiwangmu came to represent yin as Dongwanggong represents yang.

Xiwangmu was also in charge of the **elixir** of immortality. Drinking the elixir kept a person strong, active, and alive forever. Eventually, she became the wife of the Jade Emperor. She had twenty-four daughters and nine sons.

At Home in Paradise

Stories say that Xiwangmu lives on Mount Kunlun. This mythical mountain is located somewhere in the Kunlun Mountains in western China. It is a great mountain with three peaks. Xiwangmu lives at the top of the highest peak.

Myths say that Xiwangmu is surrounded by fairies and **divine** animals on her mountain. One animal is a three-legged crow.

Xiwangmu's Home

Chinese people believe that Xiwangmu lives on Mount Kunlun in the Kunlun Mountains. They consider it a holy place.

Xiwangmu, *left*, on Mount Kunlun with a peach fairy.

It is a symbol of the sun. Another one is a nine-tailed fox. It is the symbol of a long life.

Xiwangmu sits on a throne that has a tiger on one side and a dragon on the other. The tiger is a symbol of the east and the spring season. The dragon is a symbol of the west and fall. Together they represent Xiwangmu's power over the world.

PRIMARY SOURCE

Chinese scholar Liu An (180–122 BCE) described Mount Kunlun:

> He who climbs . . . onto the Hanging Garden will become a spirit; . . . He who climbs twice as high again will reach Heaven and become a god.

Source: Liu An. "Xiwangmu, the Queen Mother of the West." *University of Chicago: Humanities Division: Lucian*, Dec. 2012, lucian.uchicago.edu. Accessed 13 May 2022.

Comparing Texts

Think about the quote. Does it support the information in this chapter? Or does it give a different perspective? Explain how in a few sentences.

Xiwangmu is honored in many temples. People ask her for good health and happiness.

CHAPTER 3

Beloved by the People

Xiwangmu uses her power to help people. She gives them health, wealth, and children. She helps them escape from some of their hardships. Many people still ask Xiwangmu for help today. They visit temples and other places connected with her story.

Xiwangmu appears in a wide variety of art forms, including this jade carving that was made in the 1600s.

Xiwangmu also plays a role in many other myths. Some are the basis for festivals that are still celebrated today. In one myth, there were ten suns drying up Earth. An archer named Hou Yi shot nine of them. He then asked Xiwangmu to give him an elixir of immortality. But Hou Yi's wife, Chang'e, drank it instead. Then she rose to the moon. Chang'e became the spirit of the moon.

Xiwangmu's stories have made an impact beyond China. She is featured, *right*, in this Japanese painting from the 1770s.

A popular goddess, Xiwangmu is worshipped by many people.

Displaying Her Beauty

In art, Xiwangmu appears as a very beautiful woman. She is often shown within her palace on Mount Kunlun. Sometimes she is accompanied by servants and other goddesses. In some paintings, she is in her peach orchard. She may also appear with peaches and peach blossoms.

Bird of Hope

In mythology, the phoenix is a very beautiful bird. In some stories, it would die in a fire but then rise again. Like Xiwangmu, it represents good fortune, long life, and abundance. The phoenix goes with Xiwangmu as she takes care of the peaches. She usually wears an image of a phoenix in her headdress too.

Xiwangmu celebrates her birthday with festive events on Mount Kunlun.

Xiwangmu's birthday is another subject of Chinese art. Paintings show celebrations of her birthday on Mount Kunlun. They show large groups of immortals, musicians, animals, and attendants visiting the goddess on her birthday. Today, many Chinese people still celebrate Xiwangmu's birthday on the third day of the third lunar month. Dancers wear traditional costumes and perform in official ceremonies.

Xiwangmu is one of the most well-known Chinese goddesses. She is worshipped by people of all classes. She represents not only immortality but also happiness on earth.

Further Evidence

Look at the website below. Does it give any new evidence to support Chapter Three?

What Is a Phoenix?

abdocorelibrary.com/xiwangmu

LEGENDARY FACTS

Xiwangmu is a beautiful goddess who lives on the top of Mount Kunlun.

She takes care of the orchard where the Peaches of Immortality grow.

Every 3,000 years, she holds a feast for immortals. They eat the peaches and renew their immortality.

Xiwangmu blesses people with health, wealth, and children.

Glossary

ancestor

a person who lived long ago from whom more recent family members descend

calamity

an event that causes great harm, pain, or destruction

cultural

having to do with the way of life of a group of people; includes traditions, beliefs, and art

divine

having to do with gods or goddesses

elixir

a liquid mixture used as a medicine; often, it refers to a substance that prolongs life forever

immortals

beings who live forever

Online Resources

To learn more about Xiwangmu and Chinese mythology, visit our free resource websites below.

Visit **abdocorelibrary.com** or scan this QR code for free Common Core resources for teachers and students, including vetted activities, multimedia, and booklinks, for deeper subject comprehension.

Visit **abdobooklinks.com** or scan this QR code for free additional online weblinks for further learning. These links are routinely monitored and updated to provide the most current information available.

Learn More

Fu, Shelley. *Chinese Myths and Legends: The Monkey King and Other Adventures.* Tuttle, 2018.

Lee, Jean Kuo. *Chang'e: Goddess of the Moon.* Abdo, 2023.

Index

About the Author

Samantha S. Bell lives in the foothills of the Blue Ridge Mountains with her family and lots of cats. She is the author of more than 130 nonfiction books for kids.